HOME FRONT

Greg Owens

BROADWAY PLAY PUBLISHING INC
New York
www.broadwayplaypublishing.com
info@broadwayplaypublishing.com

HOME FRONT

Cover image by Candace Cole
First printing: August 2006
I S B N: 978-0-88145-309-6

Book design: Marie Donovan
Word processing: Microsoft Word
Typographic controls: Ventura Publisher
Typeface: Palatino
Printed and bound in the U S A

HOME FRONT was developed in part through the Downstage Left development program at Stage Left Theatre, Chicago. It received a workshop production (John Sanders, Producer) there on 17 April 2005. The cast and creative contributors were:

JO .... Janet Brooks
DARWIN .... Kurt Ehrmann
RONNIE .... Geoff Rice
LINCOLN .... Tom Hickey
LUCY .... Jameela Aghili

Director ....Shade Murray
Assistant director .... Alyson Roux

thanks to Nabil Abdelfattah, PhD for the Arabic translation on page 37

CHARACTERS & SETTING

JOSEPHINE DODGE SMITH, (JO), *fifty, a community college professor*

DARWIN SMITH, *fifty-four, a systems analyst,* JO*'s husband*

COMMANDER ABRAHAM LINCOLN, *Central Security*

RONALD REAGAN SMITH (RONNIE), *seventeen, son of* DARWIN & JO

LUCY, *a young woman*

Time: The recent past.

Place: The Smith family home

There is no intermission.

"You only are what you believe."
Phil Ochs

for our children

(Scene: The set represents the living room and kitchen of the Smith family home in a middle-class suburb of a small American city.)

(There is a sofa and a television set, with a couple of chairs and a coffee table in the living room.)

(The kitchen is upstage of the living room, divided from it by an island/counter so that one can stand in the kitchen behind the counter and interact with those in the living room.)

(Just off the kitchen, there is a dining room table with four chairs.)

(There are two main entrances and exits. The door to the house lies just beyond the kitchen. S L, there is a hallway that leads to two unseen bedrooms.)

(The house is on one level, conservatively built and decorated.)

(At rise, the stage is empty.)

(Sound: A telephone rings. After a couple of rings, JO *enters. She is dressed in a conservative jacket and skirt. She has her purse over her shoulder, a cloth bag full of books in one hand, and a plastic bag from the supermarket in the other. She places these items on the kitchen counter as she crosses to the living room to answer the cordless phone.)*

JO: Hello? Hi Sis. How are you? *(She crosses back to the kitchen and puts items from the supermarket bag into the refrigerator. She starts to prepare dinner as she talks.)* Oh, we're good. Darwin's busy with work, as usual, and I'm teaching a new course. Business and Professional Speaking. *(Listens)* Well, it's not bad. I've got a couple of students who can actually stand upright and form sentences. So we'll hope for the best. *(Listens)* Ronnie's doing great. Playing baseball, of course. *(Listens)* I know. I can't believe he's going to be a senior in high school. It goes so fast. How are Jamie and Amber? *(Listens)* I see. *(Listens)* Well, that sounds like Jamie. What's Amber up to? *(Listens)* Oh. *(Changing subject)* How's Michael? *(Listens)* Good. He's still doing the thing-a-ma-jigs? *(Listens)* Sculptures. That's what I meant. *(Listens)* Well, that's great. *(Listens)* I'm not saying it like anything. I just wouldn't imagine that six-foot sunflowers made out of junk car parts would be everyone's cup of tea, that's all. *(Interrupts)* So what's new with you? Still writing? *(Listens)* That's great, Patty. Congratulations. *(Beat)* So they pay you royalties for that, right? *(Listens, frowns)* Free copy. That's nice. *(Interrupted)* What, hon? *(Listens, then evasively)* Well, I've got to get dinner started here... *(Contradicting her words with a grimace)* I'd love to hear it. *(She listens as her sister reads her a poem on the other end. Her emotions range from annoyed to angry as she listens. When she finally responds, there is a definite edge.)* So who's publishing that poem? *The al Qaeda Review? (Listens)* Well, I think you know I don't agree with insulting the President. *(Listens)* You call him a "baby killing oil junkie" and you don't think that's insulting? *(Listens)* I think we should change the subject. *(Listens)* All I know is I'd rather be fighting the terrorists over there than on the streets of Chicago— *(Talking over her)* Patty, I really don't want to— *(Listens)* Yes, Patty. It does say "thou shalt not kill." But it doesn't say "thou shalt let them blow you up." *(Listens)* Innocent people die every day, Patty. Try not to be one of them. That's the point. *(Listens)* Yes, I am a college professor. But not all of us are raging liberals. *(Listens)* Well Patty, why don't you move there if you like them so much?

*(*DARWIN *enters, dressed conservatively in white shirt, tie; carries a briefcase.)*

DARWIN: Hello.

JO: *(To* DARWIN*)* Hello dear. *(Into phone)* Darwin just got home.

DARWIN: Who are you talking to?

JO: *(To* DARWIN*)* It's my sister.

*(*DARWIN *derisively mimes smoking a joint and flashes a peace sign.)*

JO: *(Into phone)* Darwin sends his love.

*(*DARWIN *crosses to the refrigerator and gets a beer. He opens it, standing at the kitchen counter.)*

JO: Patty, I gotta go. *(Listens)* All right. You too. Bye.

*(*JO *hangs up, sighs.* DARWIN *offers her his beer. She takes a drink.)*

DARWIN: What did she want?

JO: I think she just called to try to goad me into a political argument.

DARWIN: Isn't that what she usually does?

JO: She doesn't understand that people with real jobs and lives have other things to think about.

*(*JO *goes back to preparing dinner.* DARWIN *stays at the counter and glances at an evening newspaper as he talks to* JO.*)*

DARWIN: How are the kids?

JO: Jamie's working at an organic goat dairy collective and Amber's volunteering for the Socialist party.

DARWIN: Well, at least they bought shoes and moved out of the tipi.

JO: I don't know how they even feed themselves.

DARWIN: With their hands as I remember.

JO: *(Laughs)* How was your day?

DARWIN: Fine. You?

JO: Okay. *(Beat)* What's wrong?

DARWIN: Nothing.

JO: Something happen at work?

DARWIN: They laid off some people today.

JO: You're kidding. How many?

DARWIN: Fifty.

JO: *(Trying not to sound alarmed)* Wow.

DARWIN: They're outsourcing the data entry to the Indians. *(Beat)* Red dot. Not "woo woo".

*(*JO *nods.)*

JO: Are you worried about your job?

DARWIN: *(Trying to sound convincing)* No. *(She looks at him.)* We'll be fine.

JO: We already are.

(She kisses him. He looks uncomfortable. She goes back to making dinner.)

DARWIN: Ronnie still at practice?

JO: Yes. Why don't you sit down and relax. Dinner will be ready soon.

*(*DARWIN *sits with a newspaper, reads.)*

JO: What's the war news?

DARWIN: It'll be over soon.

JO: I hope so. Then Patty can go back to writing sonnets for dead butterflies.

DARWIN: *(Chuckles)* Your sister doesn't understand how the world works. You can't bring freedom to these people with hearts and flowers. The only thing they understand or respect is force.

JO: That's exactly how I feel about my freshmen.

DARWIN: Except you don't get to discipline them with R P Gs.

JO: *(Adopting student persona)* Which is so not fair.

(They laugh.)

JO: You need another beer?

DARWIN: *(Shakes his head)* Fine. *(Pause)* So what did you decide about the carpets?

JO: The what?

DARWIN: Carpets.

*(*JO *becomes visibly tense. She tries at first to keep her tone neutral and reveal no sign of her annoyance to* DARWIN, *who can't see her face.)*

JO: I didn't.

DARWIN: You didn't what?

JO: Decide.

DARWIN: It has to be this month.

JO: I know.

DARWIN: Certificate expires.

JO: I know.

DARWIN: Well I'm just saying, we need to figure out when we're doing it, so we can schedule it and prepare.

JO: Fine.

DARWIN: Fine what?

JO: We'll schedule it.

DARWIN: When?

JO: Whenever you'd like, dear.

DARWIN: Well, you were the one who said you wanted them done.

JO: I did.

DARWIN: So I bought the gift certificate.

JO: Yes. And it was a lovely anniversary present, dear. Thanks again.

*(*DARWIN *looks up toward her. She doesn't look at him.* RONNIE *enters. He is tall and athletic, with short hair. He wears a baseball uniform, cap, glove, carries cleats over his shoulder.)*

RONNIE: Hi Mom. Hi Dad.

DARWIN: Hey Ronnie.

*(*RONNIE *crosses to the kitchen and kisses his mother.)*

JO: How was practice?

RONNIE: It was all right.

DARWIN: Throw some good stuff today?

RONNIE: Pitched four shut-out innings in our scrimmage.

DARWIN: Way to go.

JO: That's great, dear.

RONNIE: The best part was Sasha Hurley and Mindy Darling were in the stands watching.

DARWIN: Keep your head in the game, son. Never mind the girls.

RONNIE: Thinking about girls helps my game, Dad.

JO: *(To* DARWIN*)* Your son's a show off.

DARWIN: I guess he can't help being a lady's man. Gets it from his Dad.

RONNIE: *(Laughs)* Yeah right.

*(*JO *laughs.)*

DARWIN: Hey. I wasn't always a geek. I wasn't a hot-shot pitcher like you, but I turned a few heads in my day. Ask your mother.

RONNIE: As the girls were riding by in the covered wagon, you mean?

*(*RONNIE *and* JO *laugh.)*

DARWIN: Yeah, well if you ever had to ride in a covered wagon you wouldn't laugh.

*(*RONNIE *and* JO *stop laughing and look at* DARWIN*, but politely avoid acknowledging his failed retort.)*

RONNIE: What's for dinner, Mom? I'm starving.

JO: I'm making your favorite.

RONNIE: Steak and potatoes?

JO: With green beans.

RONNIE: Awesome. I'm gonna go get cleaned up.

*(*RONNIE *starts to exit. He cruises by* DARWIN*'s chair and playfully tussles with him for a moment before exiting down the back hallway.)*

JO: Wait till you hear what's for desert.

RONNIE: *(As he leaves the stage)* Apple pie?

JO: *(To herself)* You guessed it.

DARWIN: He's almost a man.

JO: He's still a boy.

(Sound: Doorbell rings.)

*(*DARWIN *rises and crosses to the door. He opens it to* COMMANDER ABRAHAM LINCOLN, *Central Security.* LINCOLN *is in uniform. He carries a thick file folder.)*

LINCOLN: Mister Darwin Smith?

DARWIN: Yes.

LINCOLN: *(Introducing himself)* Commander Abraham Lincoln, Central Security.

DARWIN: *(Shaking* LINCOLN*'s hand)* Pleased to meet you, Commander.

LINCOLN: May I come in?

DARWIN: Of course.

*(*DARWIN *shows him in.)*

LINCOLN: This is my wife Jo.

*(*JO *crosses, shakes* LINCOLN*'s hand.)*

JO: Hello.

LINCOLN: Good evening, ma'am.

JO: I wasn't sure I heard you correctly. What did you say your name was again?

LINCOLN: Commander Abraham Lincoln.

JO: Oh. Like the president.

LINCOLN: Of course I like the President. Why wouldn't I?

JO: No, I meant—

LINCOLN: What kind of a question is that?

JO: I was just commenting—

LINCOLN: I like the President very much. Don't you?

JO: I do.

LINCOLN: You do?

JO: I do.

LINCOLN: *(To* DARWIN*)* And you?

DARWIN: I do too.

LINCOLN: All right then.

DARWIN: What can we do for you, Commander?

LINCOLN: Could we sit down?

DARWIN: Certainly.

(They all sit at the dining room table.)

JO: Coffee, Commander? Water?

LINCOLN: No. Thank you. Mister and Mrs Smith, I'm sure you must have some apprehensions about my being here, but let me assure you that it's not what you think.

JO: What do we think?

LINCOLN: Believe me, ma'am. I know how it is. I'm a parent too.

DARWIN: Is this something about Ronnie?

LINCOLN: Who?

DARWIN: Our son. Ronnie.

LINCOLN: You have a son?

JO: Yes.

LINCOLN: Hm. *(He makes a note of this.)* I'm actually here about your daughter.

DARWIN: Our daughter?

LINCOLN: Yes.

JO: But sir, we—

LINCOLN: Please, ma'am. I think it's best for everyone if you just let me say this.

DARWIN: I think there's been—

LINCOLN: Mr. Smith, I understand how you must be feeling right now. If I were in your shoes, I'd probably want to interrupt me too. But I must insist that you hear me out.

DARWIN: I apologize.

LINCOLN: Thank you. Now, what I'm going to tell you is going to sound incredible. You will find it difficult, if not impossible, to believe. But the first thing I need you both to understand is that your daughter is alive.

DARWIN: Sir, I—

LINCOLN: Do you understand that you are interfering with official government business when you break in like that? Now where was I?

*(*DARWIN *and* JO *are silent.)*

LINCOLN: What's the matter? Cat got your tongue? Where was I?

JO: You were saying—

DARWIN: Our daughter is alive.

LINCOLN: Right. *(He starts to continue, stops, looks at them curiously.)* Say, what's with you two anyway?

DARWIN: Sir?

LINCOLN: I tell you your daughter's alive and you have no reaction?

JO: Sir...

LINCOLN: Yes?

DARWIN: May we speak?

LINCOLN: Of course you can speak. It's a free country. Why wouldn't you be able to speak?

JO: Commander Lincoln, there's been a mistake.

DARWIN: We don't have a daughter.

LINCOLN: What?

JO: We don't have a daughter.

LINCOLN: What are you telling me?

JO: We have only one child. Our son. Ronnie.

*(*LINCOLN *looks at them both for a moment, then flips through some pages in his file.)*

LINCOLN: *(To* DARWIN*)* State your full name.

DARWIN: Darwin James Smith.

LINCOLN: Address?

DARWIN: 1372 Whitewood Drive.

LINCOLN: Occupation?

DARWIN: I'm a systems analyst.

LINCOLN: Where?

DARWIN: Systems Analysis, Incorporated.

LINCOLN: What kind of work do you do there?

DARWIN: I'm the Acting Assistant Group Leader for the Analytical Systems Division.

LINCOLN: *(To* JO*)* Full name.

JO: Josephine Dodge Smith.

*(*LINCOLN *looks at the file. There is a discrepancy.)*

LINCOLN: Dodge?

JO: Yes.

LINCOLN: Your middle name is Dodge?

JO: No. That's my maiden name.

LINCOLN: *(With suspicious accusation)* You're hyphenated?

JO: No. I just use Dodge because I prefer it to my given middle name.

LINCOLN: Which is?

JO: *(Reluctantly)* Millicent.

LINCOLN: *(This matches file)* Right. And what do you do?

JO: I'm a college professor.

*(*LINCOLN *frowns, raises an eyebrow.)*

JO: I teach business.

*(*LINCOLN *sees this in file, nods approvingly.)*

LINCOLN: Good. Well, the information you've just given me matches everything I have in this file. So if there's a mistake, I don't think it's me.

DARWIN: *(Laughs nervously)* But sir, don't you think we'd know if we had a daughter?

LINCOLN: My records indicate that you do.

JO: Well then, your records are incorrect.

*(*LINCOLN *reacts as if he's just been slapped in the face. He closes the folder and shows it to* JO.*)*

LINCOLN: Do you know what this is?

JO: A file folder.

LINCOLN: This is an official Central Security file folder. And do you know what's inside it?

JO: Documents?

LINCOLN: Official Central Security documents. And do you know what that means? That means this is an official Central Security file. And therefore, it is, by definition, not incorrect. Now, you say you don't have a daughter. The government says you do. Who do you expect me to believe?

*(*DARWIN *and* JO *look at one another, bewildered, silent.)*

LINCOLN: So. If I may continue: Corporal Smith's unit was traveling through the desert when they came upon two trucks parked beside the road. A small group of irregulars was standing in front of the trucks waving white flags, indicating surrender. But when Lucy's unit stopped to investigate the situation, members of the insurgents who were hidden opened fire on them and a mortar shell destroyed one of our vehicles.

DARWIN: They were ambushed.

LINCOLN: That's right. And in the fighting that ensued, five of our soldiers were killed and seven others were taken prisoner.

JO: And Lucy?

LINCOLN: She was among the P O Ws.

(There is a pause. LINCOLN *looks at both of them, expecting them to react. After a moment,* DARWIN *and* JO *get it. They react.)*

LINCOLN: At this point, I want to make clear that at no time during her imprisonment was Lucy raped or otherwise physically abused.

JO: She escaped?

LINCOLN: She was rescued. Two days after the ambush, satellite intel located the insurgents at a remote farmhouse. A Delta team was sent in to extract the prisoners.

JO: Where is she now?

LINCOLN: Before I get to that, there's something that I need to you both to understand. As you no doubt know, there have been considerable technological advancements in many areas of the military in the past thirty years. Revolutionary advancements in fact. Not only in terms of weapons and communications systems, but in medical technology as well. After she was rescued, our doctors were able to save Lucy's life using a procedure that very few people even know exists.

JO: What do you mean save her life? I thought you said she wasn't hurt.

LINCOLN: Moments before the Delta team arrived on the scene...the insurgents... *(He looks at them both seriously.)* Lucy was beheaded.

(Now the reaction is real:)

DARWIN & JO: Oh my God!

(There is a moment of stunned silence.)

JO: But you said she was alive.

LINCOLN: That's correct. You may not have heard about this, but in the early 1980s, a neurologist at M I T named Doctor Bertram Black performed a groundbreaking experiment in which he was able to transplant the head of one monkey onto another's body.

JO: Monkeys?

LINCOLN: Yes ma'am. Monkeys. For the past two decades, this technology has been developed and refined through a top-secret program called Operation Hydra. Five weeks ago, Lucy underwent the first successful human C R S—

(They look at him blankly.)

LINCOLN: —cranial reattachment surgery.

DARWIN: Are you telling us they sewed her head back on?

LINCOLN: I know it sounds fantastic. It stretches the wildest limits of our imagination. But just a few years ago, the same could have been said about heart transplants. It sounds like science fiction. But it is fact. A Medivac unit accompanying the Delta extraction team was able to place Lucy's head and body in a specially designed cryogenic field pack. She was immediately airlifted to a secret facility where our doctors performed the operation.

DARWIN: Unbelievable.

LINCOLN: Your tax dollars at work, sir. And the even better news is we're bringing Lucy home.

DARWIN: You're bringing her here?

LINCOLN: That's correct.

JO: Our daughter?

LINCOLN: Yes ma'am. Her physical recovery has so far exceeded that of any previous experimental subject. But the psychological aspects of what she's been through are tremendous, and the psychiatrists feel the family bond may play a crucial role in restoring Corporal Smith to full capacity.

DARWIN: Hold on. You can't bring her here.

LINCOLN: I beg your pardon?

JO: He doesn't mean that the way it sounds.

DARWIN: My wife and I both work. We're not prepared to take care of someone in her condition.

LINCOLN: Sir, I have to tell you that, as a father, and as a patriot, I find your attitude most offensive.

JO: I think we're both just a little overwhelmed, Commander.

LINCOLN: I understand.

JO: When does Lucy get to come home?

LINCOLN: Before we get to that, there's a matter of grave importance that I must address. The technology I've just described is essential to our security. The ability to save the lives of our soldiers, even under the most savagely inhumane circumstances the enemy can inflict, will be an extraordinary deterrent. It can completely negate the psychological impact of one of the terrorists' most potent weapons. Additionally, this technology will save the government millions of dollars. Every soldier like Lucy that we can save with this procedure is one that we don't have to replace at taxpayer expense. *(Beat)* As I said, I am a family man myself. So I don't mean for anything I say to suggest a lack of compassion or understanding. I have no doubt that the love and support of her family will contribute substantially to Corporal Smith's recovery. But let me say this: if you divulge anything about this situation to anyone under any circumstances, the consequences will be extreme.

JO: Meaning what?

*(*LINCOLN *opens file, look inside.)*

LINCOLN: I see from my records that you served in Vietnam, Mister Smith.

DARWIN: Yes.

LINCOLN: Then you understand the importance of following orders.

DARWIN: Yes sir.

LINCOLN: Freedom and Liberty are at stake, Mister and Mrs Smith. No one can know anything.

JO: When can we see her?

LINCOLN: I can bring her in now if you'd like.

DARWIN: She's here?

LINCOLN: Yes sir. She's waiting outside with a couple of my men. *(Stands)* I'll be back in a moment. Excuse me.

*(*LINCOLN *exits through the door.)*

*(*JO *gets up and crosses toward the door.* DARWIN *follows her.)*

DARWIN: What are we going to do?

JO: *(Shrugs)* Adopt?

DARWIN: This is serious, Jo. I don't want to get involved in this.

JO: He's pushing her up the walk. I think we're already involved.

DARWIN: We can't accept responsibility for this person.

JO: What choice do we have?

DARWIN: We could end up being liable for medical bills and God knows what.

JO: The man just threatened us, Darwin. What do you think he'll do if we say we won't take her?

DARWIN: But she's a total stranger.

JO: Lucy didn't care that you were a stranger when she went over there to fight for your freedom.

DARWIN: Are you questioning my patriotism?

JO: I'm questioning your compassion. Lucy needs us.

DARWIN: She needs her parents.

JO: Then we'll find them.

DARWIN: The government should be the ones to find them.

JO: Yes, except he's the government and I don't think he could find his ass with a map.

DARWIN: Keep your voice down.

(The door opens. LINCOLN *enters pushing* LUCY *in a wheelchair. He still carries the file and now also has a small pill box with different compartments divided by days of the week.)*

*(*LUCY *wears a uniform. Her head is completely covered in bandages.* JO *kneels beside the wheelchair and takes* LUCY*'s hand.)*

JO: Hello Lucy.

*(*LUCY *becomes agitated and pushes* JO*'s hand away.* JO *looks hurt.)*

LINCOLN: You must understand, Mrs Smith. It may take some time for Lucy to readjust to her surroundings.

*(*JO *nods.* RONNIE *enters, still in baseball uniform.)*

RONNIE: Hey Mom. Dinner ready yet? *(He sees* LINCOLN *and* LUCY.*)* Oh. Hi. *(To* DARWIN*)* Who's this?

JO: This is Commander Lincoln, dear. *(To* LINCOLN*)* Our son, Ronnie.

DARWIN: Ronald Reagan Smith.

LINCOLN: Like the president.

DARWIN: Yes sir, we do.

LINCOLN: It's a pleasure to meet you, son. I like that name.

RONNIE: Thank you, sir. *(To* DARWIN, *indicating* LUCY*)* Who's that?

JO: Good news, Ronnie. Your sister's home.

RONNIE: What?

LINCOLN: How old are you, Ronnie?

RONNIE: Seventeen.

LINCOLN: Play baseball?

RONNIE: Yes sir.

LINCOLN: You a good team player?

RONNIE: I guess.

DARWIN: He is, sir.

LINCOLN: That's good.

RONNIE: What's going on?

DARWIN: Your sister Lucy, Ron. She's home.

RONNIE: What are you guys talking about?

JO: Your sister Lucy is home from the war, Ronnie. She's been injured. But she's going to be all right.

RONNIE: I don't have a sister.

*(*LINCOLN *looks at him. There is an awkward moment, then* DARWIN *and* JO *both laugh.)*

DARWIN: *(To* LINCOLN*)* Our son has a strange sense of humor.

RONNIE: No I don't. Who is this?

JO: Ronnie, I understand. It's traumatic for all of us. Why don't you just go back to your room until the Commander leaves and we'll explain everything.

RONNIE: Explain what? How I suddenly have a sister I never knew about?

DARWIN: *(Sharply)* Ronnie! Now that's enough. If you don't go back to your room this minute, I'm going to beat you.

RONNIE: *(Stunned)* Dad!

DARWIN: I mean it! Now go.

RONNIE: All right. Jesus.

JO: *(Admonishing him)* Ronnie!

*(*RONNIE *sulks angrily back to his room.)*

DARWIN: *(To* LINCOLN*)* I don't like to do that. But sometimes physical intimidation is all these kids respond to.

LINCOLN: It's a father's job.

DARWIN: Yes sir.

JO: *(To* LUCY*)* Welcome home, dear. Doesn't everything look just like you remember it?

*(*LUCY *is upset.)*

JO: There, there, dear. It's all right. Mommy and Daddy are here now. It's all fine. We love you. Isn't that right, Darwin?

*(*DARWIN *looks at her like she's crazy.)*

JO: Isn't that right, dear?

DARWIN: Right.

JO: Tell her.

DARWIN: Jo—

JO: Tell your daughter that you love her.

DARWIN: I love you...

JO: Lucy.

DARWIN: Lucy.

*(*LINCOLN *takes some papers out of his file. He places them on the dining room table.)*

LINCOLN: Lucy is to remain with you for a trial period of one week. Our people will be around periodically to monitor her progress. But, for obvious reasons, you won't be able to take her outside under any circumstances.

JO: What if something happens?

LINCOLN: Call the number I'm leaving you with the documents. I can be here within minutes.

DARWIN: Where will you be?

LINCOLN: *(Cryptically)* I'll be close. *(Indicating the pill box)* These are her medications. Instructions are enclosed in the documents. If Lucy exhibits any signs of physical or mental complication, I want you to call me immediately. At the end of the week, the situation will be evaluated to determine the efficacy of Corporal Smith's domestic reinsertion and we will let you know how much longer, if at all, she is to remain at home.

DARWIN: So she's not staying.

LINCOLN: Only as long as this environment is conducive to the successful progress of this experiment. As soon as she is psychologically and physically able, she will return to the front.

JO: After everything she's been through?

LINCOLN: Ma'am—

JO: Why?

LINCOLN: I can't tell you that.

JO: Can't or won't?

DARWIN: Jo.

LINCOLN: *(Produces more papers)* If I could just get you both to sign here.

DARWIN: What's this for?

LINCOLN: To document and verify your receipt of your daughter.

JO: You said Lucy was the first successful patient. How many were there before her?

*(*LINCOLN *doesn't respond.)*

JO: What happened to them?

LINCOLN: They performed a heroic service for their country.

*(*DARWIN *and* JO *sign the document.)*

LINCOLN: The bandages can come off in three days. Not before. Understood?

DARWIN: Sir, yes, sir.

*(*LINCOLN *looks at* JO.*)*

JO: Good evening, Commander.

LINCOLN: Call me if there is any problem.

DARWIN: Yes sir. We will.

*(*LINCOLN *takes a medal out of his pocket. He crosses to* LUCY.*)*

LINCOLN: This is for you, Corporal. There will be an official ceremony later. *(Pinning it on* LUCY*)* But for now, soldier, allow me to present this to you on behalf of a grateful nation. *(He salutes her. He seems to have a moment of emotion, then quickly covers. He points at* LUCY, *addresses* DARWIN *and* JO.*)* Be proud.

*(*LINCOLN *exits.* JO *crosses to* LUCY. *She touches her on the shoulder.* LUCY *moves herself away in the chair.)*

JO: Lucy, my name is Jo. And this is Darwin. We're going to help you find your family.

*(*JO *looks at* DARWIN, *wanting him to speak.)*

DARWIN: Hello.

JO: You're safe here.

*(*LUCY *tugs at the medal on her chest, but she is too weak to pull it off. She collapses back into the chair.)*

(Blackout)

Scene Two

(Lights up on RONNIE *and* LUCY *in the living room.* LUCY *is still in her wheelchair.* RONNIE *sits in one of the living room chairs. There is a sheet, blanket, and pillow on the couch where someone has been sleeping.* LUCY *holds a cup of water with a straw in it.)*

RONNIE: So you were in the shit, huh? *(*LUCY *doesn't react.)* Cool. D'you see a lot of action? *(No reaction)* I mean before you... *(Pause)* I'm thinking about enlisting myself. If I don't get a baseball scholarship. I'd wanna be on the front lines. Get in the real shit, y'know? *(No reaction)* Can't you talk? *(No reaction)* I don't know if you can even understand a word I'm saying. *(No reaction)* My dad was a fighter pilot in Vietnam. Flew over two hundred missions. He bombed the crap outta those Commie gooks. They gave him a medal too. I'd show it to ya, but I don't know for sure where he keeps it. *(Pause)* Dad always says that going to war is the most intense experience he thinks a human being can have. It pushes you to all your limits. Body, mind, and soul. Is that how you felt? *(No reaction)* I'm intense. I don't think war's anything I couldn't handle. I thrive on pressure. And I'm at my best under challenging conditions. That's why I didn't mind giving up my room to you. Sleeping on the couch is nothing. I spent a month at a wilderness camp in Idaho one time, y'know? *(No reaction)* Well, actually it wasn't a camp. It was more of a... program. One of those places they send you when you get in trouble so you can learn discipline and teamwork and self-control and all that shit. *(Beat)* I had to go there after I kicked the shit out of this kid at school. He didn't really do anything to me. So it was kinda wrong. I just did it really for fun. He was a total fag. So he sorta had it coming. I guess I shouldn't have done it though. That kind of thing looks bad on your record when you're applying for college. *(No reaction)* At this camp they taught us how to dig latrines and set signal fires and make snares to catch rabbits and hunt berries and roots and shit. We learned a lot of cool shit. It was pretty tough. We also had to do a lot of hiking. With forty pounds of gear on our backs. *(Beat)* I think I could handle war. Don't you?

(LUCY *slowly turns her head and looks toward the kitchen.* RONNIE *notices this.)*

RONNIE: Oh, Mom'll be back in a minute. She just had to run to the store and pick up a couple of things for dinner. She's a good cook. She makes the best steak and potatoes in the whole state. She's smart too. She's a teacher. And pretty. I think she's about the best-looking mom outta all the guys I know at school. Sometimes one of the guys at school will make a crack about my mom. About how good-looking she is. I don't mind if they're just kidding around. But if it goes too far, I let 'em know. I'll kick the shit outta them. They know that. I love my mom. *(Beat)* I love my Dad too. But I don't say that around him because, you know, I don't want him to think I'm weak. He's got a good job. I don't really know what he does but it's important. He makes money. What about your parents? *(No reaction)* Where do they live? What do they do? My mom's been trying to find them for ya. It'd sure help if you'd talk. Tell us where they are. I'm sure they'd be worried about you. I mean, unless they're some kind of white-trash shitbags or something. I hear a lot of those kinds of kids end up going into the military because they don't have any money or opportunities or anything. So unless they wanna end up working in some factory and living in a trailer the rest of their lives, married to their cousins, with fourteen dogs and a half a dozen kids, they figure they're better off dodging a few bullets for Uncle Sam.

(No reaction) I wish I could be over there right now. M-16. Couple of grenades. Bazooka maybe. I'd show those raghead motherfuckers what they get for messing with us.

*(*LUCY *holds out her drink cup and shakes it.)*

RONNIE: You need some more water there? I'll get it for you.

*(*RONNIE *gets up and crosses to her. He reaches for the cup.* LUCY *throws water in his face.)*

RONNIE: Hey, what the hell'd you do that for? That's not cool.

*(*LUCY *throws the cup on the floor.* RONNIE *stares at her.)*

*(*JO *enters, carrying a grocery bag.)*

JO: Hello! How's the family?

*(*RONNIE *crosses to the kitchen to complain to his mother.)*

RONNIE: Mom, she just threw water in my face.

JO: What?

RONNIE: I was gonna get her another glass of water and she threw it my face.

(Concerned, JO *crosses to* LUCY.*)*

JO: Is everything all right, dear? Did something happen to upset you?

RONNIE: What are you talking about? She threw water at me. I'm the one who's upset.

JO: Ronnie, I've told you. You have to be patient with Lucy. She's been through a traumatic experience.

RONNIE: But I didn't do anything.

JO: *(To* LUCY*)* Now Lucy, you really must make an effort to be nicer to Ronnie. He's trying to help you.

RONNIE: I don't think she can talk.

JO: She'll talk when she's ready.

RONNIE: I don't know. Maybe she's not right. Maybe they scrambled some of her brains up when they whacked her head off.

JO: Ronnie! Don't talk that way in front of Lucy. You'll upset her.

RONNIE: She doesn't look upset. She's just sitting there.

JO: That will be enough. Why don't you go outside?

RONNIE: When's dinner? I'm starving.

JO: Dinner will be ready soon. Now go.

RONNIE: Fine. *(To* LUCY*)* Nice talking to you. Not.

*(*RONNIE *exits.)*

JO: Don't pay any attention to him, dear. Ronnie's a good boy, but sometimes he has maturity issues. I think it's because I didn't breast-feed. Darwin says that's crazy, but I don't know. Now, why don't you come over here and keep me company.

*(*JO *pushes* LUCY *over closer to the kitchen.* JO *takes a cup of yogurt out of the grocery bag. She peels off the lid and gets a spoon from one of the drawers.)*

JO: I got you some more yogurt. Do you think you could feed yourself while I get dinner ready? *(She puts the yogurt and the spoon in* LUCY*'s hands.)* There you go, dear. It's your favorite. Blueberry banana. *(She goes back to work in the kitchen.)* I'm afraid it's nothing fancy tonight. Just some sausages and sauerkraut I picked up at the store. Does that sound okay? *(No reaction)* I wish you'd say something, Lucy. I can't even tell if you're understanding a word I say. *(Beat)* I made a few calls on my lunch break trying to track down your parents. No luck so far. There are a lot of Smiths. But I have a couple of leads. We'll find them for you, dear. You needn't worry. It would be easier though if you could give me some information. Their first names or where you're from. *(No reaction)* I always wanted a daughter, you know. I love my Ronnie. Don't get me wrong. He's absolutely perfect in every way. But I always thought it would be nice to have a little girl. Someone I could buy pretty dresses for and put ribbons in her hair. Did you like pretty dresses when you were a little girl? *(No reaction)* Darwin didn't want another child. I don't know why. He'd never really say. Oh, he'd make excuses. It would cost too much. We'd have to get a bigger house. But I don't think that was it really. I think it had something to do with his experiences in the war. He's never really talked about it, but I know that he was quite troubled for a long time after he came home. That was before I knew him. But even after we were married, he used to have nightmares sometimes. Wake up screaming awful things and crying. Like you. *(No reaction)* He was terrified when Ronnie was born. I mean he loved him. He's always loved him. In his way. And I know he's proud of him. But I think something about fatherhood really frightened him. The vulnerability. I don't think he could've gone through it a second time. *(Beat)* I'm sure your parents must be extremely proud of you. What you've done for your country. You're a bona fide hero. Or heroine I guess. That medal on your chest proves it. *(Pause)* I've sometimes wondered—I'd never say this to Darwin—but I've had my doubts, occasionally, whether this war was really a good thing. *(No reaction)* I can't tell you how much I admire your courage.

*(*LUCY *throws the yogurt and the spoon toward* JO. *The spoon barely misses her. Yogurt goes everywhere.)*

JO: Oh now, Lucy. What did you have to do that for? That wasn't very nice. *(She gets a towel from the sink and starts to clean up the mess.)* Wasteful too. There are people in the world who are starving you know?

Women and children who'd be happy to crawl around this kitchen and lick that yogurt off the floor. That's how hungry they are. And here you go just throwing it away.

*(*LUCY *turns her head away.)*

JO: I'm not upset with you. I know you didn't mean it.

*(*DARWIN *enters carrying a briefcase.)*

DARWIN: What the hell...

JO: *(Still cleaning up)* How was your day?

DARWIN: What happened here?

JO: Lucy had a little accident with her yogurt.

DARWIN: An accident?

JO: She just spilled it.

DARWIN: All over the kitchen?

JO: It's nothing. No harm done.

DARWIN: What's for dinner?

JO: I'm afraid it's just sausages and sauerkraut tonight, dear. Is that okay?

DARWIN: *(It's not really)* Fine.

JO: Everything go okay at the office?

DARWIN: Sure. Except for the accounting department.

JO: More layoffs?

DARWIN: Apparently the Indians can add too.

JO: Darwin, are we okay?

DARWIN: Is Ronnie home? Why don't we eat out tonight.

JO: He's outside. But we can't do that.

DARWIN: Why not?

JO: *(To* LUCY*)* Why don't we take you over here by the window for a minute, dear. *(She pushes* LUCY *over to the window and returns to* DARWIN.*)* We can't take her out to a restaurant. What are you thinking?

DARWIN: She can stay here.

JO: We can't leave her alone.

DARWIN: She was alone all day wasn't she?

JO: No. Of course not.

*(*DARWIN *looks at her, doesn't understand.)*

JO: Ronnie was with her.

*(*JO *gets plates, etc. ready and puts them on the table as they talk.* DARWIN *is not happy about what she's just said.)*

JO: Just for today.

DARWIN: So now you've got Ronnie missing baseball practice, possibly jeopardizing his future, to stay here and be a nursemaid to that girl.

JO: That girl's name is Lucy. And I told you it was just for one day.

DARWIN: What are we going to do tomorrow? And the day after that?

JO: Tomorrow is Saturday, dear. And I've spoken to my dean. He's going to get someone else to take over my classes for the next week.

DARWIN: You're taking the whole week off?

JO: It's not a problem.

DARWIN: Jo, we can't go on like this. This girl needs more help than we can give her.

JO: Her name is Lucy.

DARWIN: I don't care what her name is. Listen to me. This isn't going to work. We've got to call Lincoln.

(Without DARWIN *and* JO *noticing,* LUCY *slowly lifts herself up out of the wheelchair and stands. Throughout the next section of dialogue, she walks slowly toward the front door.)*

JO: I just need a little more time to find her family.

DARWIN: I think it's more important to protect our family.

JO: You can't think she's dangerous.

DARWIN: You don't know what combat can do to a person, Jo. I do. It's horrible what's happened to this woman. But they never should have brought her back from that kind of Hell.

JO: I'm sure her family will be glad she's alive.

DARWIN: But will she?

*(*LUCY *is just behind* DARWIN *and* JO*, and almost to the door, when her strength fails and she collapses onto the floor.* DARWIN *and* JO *are both startled.* JO *goes to help her.)*

JO: Oh my goodness. Let me help you, darling. Look at you. On your feet. That's wonderful, Lucy. Look, Darwin. She was walking. Isn't that wonderful?

*(*DARWIN *doesn't respond.)*

JO: Why don't you call Ronnie for dinner and I'll help Lucy over to the table.

*(*DARWIN *crosses to the hallway.* JO *takes* LUCY *by the arm.)*

JO: Come on, dear. One step at a time.

DARWIN: Ronnie!

RONNIE: *(O S)* Yeah Dad.

DARWIN: Dinner.

JO: *(As she walks* LUCY *to her chair)* That's it. Just like learning it all over again.

*(*RONNIE *enters. He and* DARWIN *cross to the table and sit.* JO *helps* LUCY *into her chair.* JO *sits in the chair next to her.)*

JO: Now, let me cut up these sausages for you.

*(*JO *takes a knife and fork and cuts up the meat.)*

RONNIE: Hey Dad, remember we've got a game tomorrow. You gonna come?

DARWIN: Sure I am. Wouldn't miss it.

*(*DARWIN *makes eye contact with* RONNIE, *nods toward* JO, *indicating that* RONNIE *should invite her too.)*

RONNIE: What do you say, Mom? Wanna come?

*(*JO *finishes with the sausages. She sets the knife down beside* LUCY*'s plate.)*

JO: No thank you, dear. You boys go have fun. The girls will stay here and find something to entertain ourselves. *(To* DARWIN*)* Would you say grace, please?

(They all reach for one another's hands. JO *and* RONNIE, *who are sitting closest to* LUCY, *try to take her hands.* LUCY *resists.* RONNIE *lets go of her hand.)*

RONNIE: Whatever.

JO: *(To* LUCY*)* It's all right, dear. We're just going to say a prayer.

*(*LUCY *relents and lets them hold her hands.* DARWIN, JO, *and* RONNIE *bow their heads and close their eyes.)*

DARWIN: Thank you Lord for your many blessings and thank you for this food that we are about to enjoy. We pray that you will watch over us and guide us. In—

*(*JO *squeezes* DARWIN*'s hand. He opens his eyes and looks at her. She nods her head toward* LUCY, *wanting him to say something about her.)*

DARWIN: We also thank you, Lord, for bringing Lucy safely back home and we pray that you will help her be reunited with her family. Very soon. In Jesus' name we pray. Amen.

RONNIE & JO: Amen.

JO: Well then—

(Just as the family is about to dig in, LUCY *suddenly grabs the knife. She rises to her feet and jabs the knife into the table, just inches from* JO*'s hand. All react with silent shock, staring at the knife stuck into the table.)*

(Blackout)

Scene Three

(Lights up on JO *in the kitchen. She pours herself a cup of coffee.)*

(DARWIN *enters.)*

JO: How'd you sleep?

DARWIN: I didn't sleep, Jo. I stood guard outside her room all night.

JO: Oh.

DARWIN: We have to talk.

JO: I know what you're going to say.

DARWIN: She goes.

JO: Darwin-

DARWIN: No. Listen to me. I told you that girl was dangerous.

JO: I don't think Lucy meant to threaten us.

DARWIN: She came only inches from stabbing that knife into your hand.

JO: Lucy wasn't trying to hurt me. She was simply acting out. Like a child. That's what she is, Darwin. A scared, helpless child.

DARWIN: I'm calling Lincoln this morning. He said he wanted us to call if it seemed like there was anything wrong with her.

JO: Well, if you're so set on calling him then why haven't you done it already? Since when do you need my approval on anything?

DARWIN: We've got to put up a united front. I can't bring him in here until I know what you're going to say when he comes.

JO: So it's not that you care about my feelings, you just don't trust me.

DARWIN: Feelings have nothing to do with this.

JO: Of course not. Why should this be any different?

DARWIN: Can we please not get into all that right now?

JO: You'd better get ready. You're going to be late for your ball game.

DARWIN: I'm not going to the game.

JO: But you promised Ronnie. He'll be disappointed.

DARWIN: He'll just have to deal with that. I'm not leaving you alone in the house with that mad woman.

JO: I'm not afraid.

DARWIN: Well maybe that's because you don't have enough sense to be afraid.

JO: Don't talk to me like that.

DARWIN: I will talk to exactly like that. I know why you're doing this, Jo.

JO: If you call him, he'll take her away.

DARWIN: Honey, you're not being rational.

JO: Why am I doing this?

*(*DARWIN *doesn't answer.)*

JO: Tell me. I want to hear what you think you know about me.

DARWIN: She's not ours. We have one child. One. And that's it. That was our choice. We can't change that now.

JO: No, Darwin. That wasn't our choice. It was yours.

DARWIN: Fine. You can blame me for that till the end of our lives if you want.

JO: I will.

(She turns away from him.)

DARWIN: Josephine, can't you see that I'm only thinking about you and Ronnie? If anything happened to you—

JO: If anything happened to us, you'd go right along as always. You'd drive to work in the morning and come home at night and read your paper. Nothing would change. It wouldn't affect you in the least.

DARWIN: That isn't true. How can you think that?

JO: You've been a ghost in this house for twenty years. You pass right through me and I can't even feel you.

*(*DARWIN *is stunned. Long pause)*

JO: I won't let you take her away from me.

*(*RONNIE *enters. He wears a baseball cap and glove.)*

RONNIE: Morning, Mom. Morning, Dad.

JO: Good morning.

DARWIN: Good morning, son.

RONNIE: Hey Dad, you better get dressed. Game starts in an hour.

DARWIN: Ronnie, I'm sorry to disappoint you, but I'm afraid I won't be able to make it to the game today.

RONNIE: Why not?

DARWIN: I feel I should stay here and help your mother.

RONNIE: With what?

DARWIN: Take care of Lucy.

RONNIE: Ah, man. That's bullshit.

JO: Ronnie!

DARWIN: Watch your language.

RONNIE: You said you'd go.

DARWIN: I know I did. And I'm sorry. But not today, son. Another time.

RONNIE: I hate that bitch.

DARWIN: Now that's enough! I mean it.

RONNIE: *(To* DARWIN*)*You don't want her here either.

DARWIN: That's not true.

RONNIE: Why won't you admit it? *(Indicating* JO*)* You gonna let her tell you what to do?

DARWIN: I'm warning you.

JO: Lucy needs our help, Ronnie.

RONNIE: She doesn't appreciate it. She doesn't care. Look at everything we've done for her already and what does she do? Freaks out and goes psycho right in the middle of dinner.

JO: I think you need to show a little more respect.

RONNIE: And I think you need to wake the fuck up.

*(*DARWIN *slaps him hard across the face.)*

DARWIN: You will not talk to your mother like that.

(Pause. LUCY *enters, walking a little better.)*

JO: *(Crossing to her)* Good morning, dear. How did you sleep? Why don't you come over here and sit down and I'll make you some breakfast.

*(*JO *tries to lead* LUCY *to the table.* LUCY *pushes her away.* LUCY *loses her balance on the way to the table and* JO *helps her sit.* JO *makes eye contact with* DARWIN *and indicates that she wants him to speak to* LUCY.*)*

DARWIN: Good morning, Lucy.

*(*JO *does the same to* RONNIE. *He ignores her and throws himself down on the couch.)*

JO: But before we eat, I've got a little surprise for you, Lucy. I think it's time to take off your bandages.

*(*DARWIN *reacts.)*

JO: I think it will help you feel more comfortable if you can see us and your surroundings.

DARWIN: You can't do that. Not till tomorrow. That's what Lincoln said.

JO: What difference does it make?

DARWIN: Because that's what he said, Jo. He said three days.

JO: Well, Commander Lincoln isn't here now and I say they should come off today.

DARWIN: But what if he comes by?

JO: Then he comes by.

DARWIN: We could get in a lot of trouble if we disobey his orders.

JO: I don't take orders from him. I am a mother. And I know what it is best for my children.

DARWIN: Jo, she's not your child.

*(*JO *ignores him, moves toward* LUCY. RONNIE *looks at* DARWIN *to see if he will stop her.* DARWIN *does not. He avoids looking at* RONNIE. *They both watch* JO.*)*

JO: All right, dear. Nice and easy now. I'm going to try not to hurt you. I bet you can't wait to get these off.

(As JO *begins to unwrap the bandages,* LUCY *resists.)*

JO: So many beautiful things to see. The birds in the trees and the blue sky. Sunlight on the grass. Flowers in bloom. Soft pink babies at their mothers' breasts.

*(*LUCY *pushes* JO*'s hands away again.)*

JO: The world is full of beautiful things, Lucy. It's time for you to remember that.

(As JO *unwraps the bandages, a head of curly black hair becomes visible.)*

JO: My, what lovely dark hair you have. It's funny. Somehow I'd been imagining you as a blonde.

*(*LUCY *pushes* JO *away and begins to unwrap the bandages herself. As parts of the face become visible, it is clear that the skin tone is darker than that of her hands and arms.* RONNIE *and* DARWIN *start to notice this.)*

JO: There you go.

*(*LUCY *pulls away the last of the bandages and the face is, at last revealed.)*

JO: Hello my girl. Welcome.

*("*LUCY*" looks at them as they all stare at the scar on her neck where her Arabic head has been attached to the body of a white woman.* LUCY *stands. She speaks to them in Arabic:)*

"LUCY": *'undhuru jayyidan, ya 'asdiqaa'i-l 'amriikiyyiin, 'ila silaahikum 'assirriy (Take a good look, my American friends...at your secret weapon.)*

*(They react with shock at the sound of her voice. "*LUCY*" stares back at them.)*

(Blackout)

Scene Four

(Lights up. DARWIN *and* JO *are sitting in the living room with* LINCOLN *between them.* RONNIE *hovers nearby. "*LUCY*" sits in the wheel chair.* LINCOLN *looks at "*LUCY,*" then back at* DARWIN *and* JO.*)*

LINCOLN: I'm afraid I don't see the problem.

(There is a pause. The SMITH *family looks at him in disbelief.)*

RONNIE: You got the wrong head.

*(*LINCOLN *looks at* RONNIE, *doesn't respond.)*

RONNIE: She's a haji, for crying out loud!

JO: I won't allow you to talk about people that way in my house.

RONNIE: She's not a person.

DARWIN: Cut it out, Ron.

RONNIE: *(Defiantly)* Or what?

LINCOLN: Can someone please explain to me what this is all about?

JO: When we took the bandages off this morning—

LINCOLN: You took the bandages off this morning?

JO: Yes.

LINCOLN: Didn't I tell you not to take the bandages off until tomorrow?

JO: Yes. You did. But I—

LINCOLN: So you disobeyed a direct order?

JO: With all due respect, I don't—

LINCOLN: What were you thinking taking the bandages off today?

DARWIN: Sir, my wife realizes that she made a mistake.

JO: I realize no such thing.

DARWIN: *(To* JO*)* Please let me speak. *(To* LINCOLN*)* The main point right now is that when she did take the bandages off—

LINCOLN: Illegally—

DARWIN: Yes sir. When she took them off, this woman began shouting at us in Arabic.

LINCOLN: Arabic?

JO: Yes!

LINCOLN: What do you mean Arabic?

JO: The language.

LINCOLN: I'm aware that Arabic is a language.

DARWIN: Yes sir.

*(*LINCOLN *searches through his files.)*

LINCOLN: I see no record here of your daughter receiving language training.

JO: Use your eyes for goodness sake. You can see for yourself that this woman's head doesn't belong to her body. It's obvious that something has gone horribly wrong here.

LINCOLN: Well, I think I know why. I specifically instructed you not to remove the bandages until tomorrow.

JO: Are you kidding me? Are you really going to sit there and tell me that this wouldn't have happened if I'd left the bandages on for another day? What? Today her head is Arabic and tomorrow she would've been a California blonde?

LINCOLN: I don't appreciate this insubordinate behavior.

JO: I am not one of your petrified underlings that you can order about at will, Commander Lincoln. I am a free American woman and I have the right to behave any way I damn well wish inside my own home.

DARWIN: Jo, please calm down, honey.

JO: No, I will not calm down. *(To* LINCOLN*)* If your precious documents indicate that I am the mother of Lucy Smith then I, in that capacity, am telling you, the person responsible, that this is not her.

*(*LINCOLN *looks nervous.)*

JO: So my question for you, sir, and for the entire United States government is this: Where in the hell is my daughter's head?

(Pause)

"LUCY": Please don't be upset, mother.

(Everyone looks at "LUCY."*)*

LINCOLN: I thought you said she spoke Arabic.

DARWIN: She does.

LINCOLN: Well, I'm no expert, but that sounded like English to me. You wanna tell me what's going on here?

"LUCY": Sir, please don't be upset with my family, Sir. They've been through a terrible shock. They're very upset, Sir.

LINCOLN: *(Opening file)* State your full name.

"LUCY": Sir, Corporal Lucy Anne Smith, Sir.

LINCOLN: Are these people your family?

"LUCY": Sir, yes, Sir.

LINCOLN: Then can you explain why they would want to deny their connection to you?

"LUCY": I'm not sure, sir. But I believe it may be related to my decision to join the military.

DARWIN: What?

"LUCY": *(To* LINCOLN*)* My family wasn't happy with this choice. They didn't want me to enlist, sir. They don't support the war.

DARWIN: I won't sit here and listen to these damn lies.

"LUCY": My brother Ronnie has said that only poor white trash with no education join the military.

RONNIE: I never said that!

*(*JO *takes* RONNIE*'s arm, tries to calm him down.)*

"LUCY": My mother told me that she didn't think that this war was a good thing.

("LUCY" *avoids making eye contact with* JO*, who stares at her intently.* JO *looks like she feels more betrayed than angry.)*

"LUCY": And my father says the government should have let me die.

RONNIE: My dad's a veteran!

LINCOLN: Yes. I see that in your file, Mister Smith.

*(*DARWIN *looks uneasy.)*

RONNIE: He was a fighter pilot in Vietnam.

DARWIN: Ronnie—

RONNIE: He flew over two hundred missions.

DARWIN: Son, don't talk about that right now.

RONNIE: Why not, Dad? I want him to know you served your country.

LINCOLN: Yes. Indeed. I'd be very interested to hear about your experiences as a fighter pilot, Mister Smith.

DARWIN: Commander, please. I can explain.

LINCOLN: How many bombing missions was it? Two hundred?

RONNIE: Over two hundred.

DARWIN: Ronnie, why don't you go into the other room for a moment?

RONNIE: Why?

DARWIN: Your mother and I need to speak to Commander Lincoln in private.

RONNIE: About what?

DARWIN: Just go on, Ronnie. It doesn't concern you.

RONNIE: I've got a right to know. I'm part of this family. It does concern me.

DARWIN: We'll discuss it later, son. Please go.

LINCOLN: Actually I think Ronnie should stay for this. And your daughter too.

RONNIE: What's going on?

(LINCOLN flips some pages in the file.)

LINCOLN: Private Darwin Smith—

RONNIE: Private? What are you talking about? He was a captain.

DARWIN: *(Embarrassed)* Ronnie.

RONNIE: *(Confused)* Dad?

DARWIN: Please be quiet, son.

LINCOLN: *(Reading)* Private Smith. Drafted June 17, 1969. Deployed to South Vietnam, August 1969. Court-martialed March 2nd, 1970 for refusing to follow orders from commanding officer. Dishonorably discharged, April 12th, 1970.

RONNIE: That's not true. None of that is true. *(To* DARWIN*)* You've got to tell him that's not true.

DARWIN: Son, don't.

RONNIE: He's wrong. He was wrong about her and he's wrong about this.

DARWIN: It's the truth, Ronnie. I was lying to you before. I was never a pilot. I didn't want you to be ashamed of me.

RONNIE: You were court-martialed?

DARWIN: Yes.

JO: Why?

DARWIN: Because I refused to murder innocent civilians.

LINCOLN: Those were Viet Cong spies, Mister Smith.

DARWIN: They were women and children.

"LUCY": Commander Lincoln, I think it would be better if I left my family. I'm afraid that this environment is not conducive to my recovery and my staying here, given my family's emotional and ideological condition, may endanger our mission.

RONNIE: *(To* LINCOLN*)* There. You heard her. She wants to go. Take her.

*(*DARWIN *looks hopefully at* LINCOLN. LINCOLN *looks at* JO.*)*

JO: What if I'm right? What if she isn't Lucy Smith? What would that do to your mission?

*(*DARWIN *and* RONNIE *look angrily at* JO. LINCOLN *looks at all of them suspiciously.)*

LINCOLN: I'm going to have to consult with the other members of the committee before I—we—make a final decision.

*(*LINCOLN *stands abruptly to go.* DARWIN *glares at* JO. "LUCY" *rises from the chair.)*

"LUCY": Commander, please!

DARWIN: Come on, you can't just leave her here!

LINCOLN: *(To* DARWIN*)* You do not tell me what I can and cannot do, Private. *(Beat)* You'd better get control of this situation now.

*(*LINCOLN *exits.)*

*(*DARWIN *looks at* RONNIE, *who looks down at the floor.)*

DARWIN: Son...

*(*RONNIE *looks at* DARWIN, *hurt and very angry.* RONNIE *storms out of the room down the hallway.)*

DARWIN: *(To* JO*)* I hope you're happy now. *(He exits.)*

JO: Who are you?

NIDAL: I am Nidal.

JO: Why did you say those awful things about my family?

NIDAL: I want to go home.

JO: Well then just go. You don't have to slander us all as traitors.

NIDAL: I did not desire conflict with you. You created it.

JO: I've put my family at risk for you.

NIDAL: If you insist on convincing Lincoln that I am not Lucy Smith, you will ensure their deaths.

JO: I won't help you deceive my country.

NIDAL: Yes, I'm sure you're more comfortable with your country deceiving you.

JO: *(Angrily)* I'm sick and tired of you people blaming everything on the United States. Innocent American children have died trying to liberate your country. How do you think their parents feel? Do you have no compassion for them? Does their suffering mean nothing to you?

NIDAL: I feel compassion for the suffering of all people. My religion teaches me this.

JO: Is this the same religion that teaches you to fly airplanes into our buildings?

NIDAL: Terrorism has nothing to do with my religion.

JO: Then why is it every time I turn on the news, I see some raghead with a backpack full of dynamite blowing up a bus?

NIDAL: You see what you wish to see. Or what you are instructed to see.

JO: I see a race of people who hate and want to destroy us.

NIDAL: I am not your enemy.

JO: Prove it.

NIDAL: Why do you think your husband refused to kill innocent human beings when his government ordered him to do so?

JO: You don't know anything about my husband.

NIDAL: Are you ashamed of his choice?

JO: I'm proud of what he did. It was right.

NIDAL: I agree. This is why I tried to save Lucy Smith. *(Beat)* Her kidnappers brought her to my hospital. She was injured during her abduction and I cared for her, even though I knew that they only wished to keep her alive long enough to torture her. When they came back to take her away, I resisted them. I thought that hers was one death I could prevent. But her captors accused me of being a traitor, and I was taken along with Lucy to the place where we were both beheaded. I was unable to save her.

JO: You were a doctor.

NIDAL: I am. Josephine, please. I must go home. I need to know if my children are still alive.

JO: How old?

NIDAL: My son Salam is eight. Khalida, my daughter, is six.

JO: Where are they?

NIDAL: I don't know.

JO: You've got to tell Lincoln.

NIDAL: They will kill me.

JO: No. I don't believe that.

(DARWIN *enters. He's taking a handgun out of a plastic bag.)*

DARWIN: All right. Everybody just calm down. I'm in control here.

JO: Darwin, where did that come from?

DARWIN: I got it at Wal-Mart.

JO: When?

DARWIN: Yesterday.

JO: But you've never owned a weapon since I've known you.

(DARWIN *takes out bullets and starts to load the gun.)*

DARWIN: I know how to use it.

JO: Why do you have it?

DARWIN: Honey, I don't want you to worry. *(He crosses to* NIDAL, *points the gun at her.)* Out of the chair.

JO: What are you doing?

DARWIN: *(To* NIDAL*)* Up.

*(*NIDAL *gets out of the chair.)*

DARWIN: On your knees.

JO: Darwin, my God!

DARWIN: *(To* NIDAL*)* Now.

*(*NIDAL *kneels.)*

JO: Darwin, don't.

*(*DARWIN *stands behind* NIDAL, *looks at* JO.*)*

DARWIN: Could you get us some writing paper and a pen?

*(*JO *looks perplexed.* DARWIN *explains:*

DARWIN: You always put stuff back in different places. I never know where we keep anything.

*(*JO *crosses to the dining room, where she opens a drawer and takes out a writing tablet and a pen.)*

NIDAL: You are making a mistake, Mister Smith.

DARWIN: *(To* NIDAL*)* Don't talk.

(As JO *brings him the pad and pen)*

DARWIN: Thank you, dear. *(He puts the pad and pen on the floor in front of* NIDAL.*)* I assume you write English as well as you speak it.

NIDAL: No.

DARWIN: Well you're gonna learn.

JO: Darwin, please stop this.

DARWIN: I realize that this whole experience has brought up a lot of feelings for you, Jo. That you've been empathically involved with this woman's plight. And I don't want you to think I don't respect your feelings about this. I do.

(RONNIE *enters.)*

DARWIN: But it's important for you to understand that my responsibility as the head of this family is to decide on a course of action that best protects us and ensures our safety. And to do that, I can't be hindered by emotion. I have to think, and act, with rationality. I have to kill her. *(Noticing him)* Hey Ron.

RONNIE: Dad.

DARWIN: I'll make it look suicide. Lincoln mentioned we should watch out for depression. *(To* NIDAL*)* Start writing what I tell you.

JO: Darwin—

DARWIN: Quiet please. I have to think. *(begins dictating)* "To my precious family..."

*(*NIDAL *starts to write.* DARWIN *looks over her shoulder at the pad.* NIDAL *stops, looks confused.)*

NIDAL: How do you spell "precious"?

DARWIN: Jo?

JO: "P-R-E-C-I-O-U-S."

DARWIN: Thank you. *(Continues dictating)* "I don't know how to tell you how sorry I am for what I have done, or if I can explain my reasons. I don't want you to think that this was your fault, or that there was anything you could have done to prevent it."

*(*NIDAL *looks up at* JO.*)*

JO: "P-R-E-V-E-N-T."

DARWIN: "I have been very sad for a long time now and that has nothing to do with you. There are just some things in my past that I don't know how to deal with. But never think that you didn't make me happy. Even at this moment I smile at memories of our good times." *(Looks at* JO*)* You remember that time, when we were first going out, we had dinner at the Mexican place on Walnut Street?

JO: Yes.

(While they're talking, DARWIN *takes a shoulder holster out of the bag from the store. He takes a price tag off of it by biting the little plastic thing with his teeth. He puts it on and puts the gun in the holster.)*

DARWIN: By the time we finished dinner, it was pouring down rain. I paid the check and told you to wait in the foyer for me to bring the car around so you wouldn't get wet. I got soaked as I ran across the parking lot to my old Mustang. You remember that car?

*(*JO *smiles, nods.)*

DARWIN: As I'm putting the key in the door to unlock it, I hear your shoes on the wet pavement. I look up to see you running toward me. Like a big happy wet dog.

JO: *(Laughs)* How romantic.

*(*DARWIN *laughs, embarrassed.)*

DARWIN: I'm not saying it well. You've always been the word person, Jo.

JO: I'm sure if you could write it in code it would be beautiful.

DARWIN: My point is I can still see you so clearly in that one random moment. I can still remember exactly how I felt.

JO: Drenched?

DARWIN: Relaxed.

JO: That's nice.

DARWIN: And what has it been now, a quarter of a century? I still think about that moment every time I drive by that place.

(JO *starts to say something.)*

DARWIN: I mean it's a jiffy lube now, the restaurant's gone. But you know, that spot. It still makes me think of one of my favorite moments of you. And whenever that happens, I go around that whole day feeling good.

(JO *smiles.)*

DARWIN: I know I don't tell you often enough how much you mean to me. But what you said before was wrong. You and Ronnie are part of me. If anything ever happened to you, it would kill me.

JO: I'm sorry.

DARWIN: *(Resumes dictation)* "I have always tried to do everything that my country, my employers, and my family have expected of me. I have failed all three at one time or another, but not because I didn't care. I have tried to make every sacrifice."

RONNIE: Hey Dad, are you all right?

DARWIN: Never been better. Feels good to take the bull by the horns. Always be proactive. Remember that, son.

RONNIE: Okay.

JO: Darwin—

DARWIN: *(Resumes dictation)* "It's hard to end this life that you have all given so much to. But the truth is even the love of the greatest family in the world is not enough to lift the weight of my sorrow. I am broken and will never mend. Signed... Humpty Dumpty."

(NIDAL *looks confused.)*

RONNIE: What the hell...

JO: It was your favorite book when you were two.

DARWIN: You remember?

RONNIE: Sort of.

JO: Your dad used to read it to you.

DARWIN: The book was eight pages long and you'd ask eight hundred questions before we got through it. Who's that? Why is he Humpty Dumpty? Why is he sitting on the wall? Why did he fall? Why can't they put him back together again? Why is he an egg? That was my favorite.

RONNIE: *(Not knowing what to say)* Cool.

*(*DARWIN *sees that* NIDAL *has not signed the note.)*

DARWIN: Sign it.

JO: They'll find out, Darwin. You won't fool them.

DARWIN: *(Insulted)* Because I'm not even good enough to compete with the biggest group of fools in the world?

JO: When they read that note, they're going to know that Lucy Smith didn't write it.

DARWIN: Like they knew nothing was wrong with "Lucy Smith"?

JO: They'll know because it sounds like you.

DARWIN: Well, of course it does. I'm the one who did all the work. You're happy to criticize it now but I didn't see you volunteering to help write the suicide note.

JO: Think of what they might do to us.

DARWIN: Why? Because "Lucy Smith" is such a valuable top-secret asset? Well, if that's the case, do you think they'd ever let her see her parents in the first place? If they did, don't you think they'd have pretty tight surveillance on the place? *(He paces around the room, talking into suspected surveillance bugs.)* There'd be bugs everywhere, wouldn't you think? So if, for instance, I said I was gonna kill her, they'd hear that and come running. Wouldn't they? *(Stops, looks at* JO*)* Unless killing her is exactly what they want me to do.

NIDAL: "P-A-R-A-N-O-I-D."

DARWIN: I told you to sign it.

JO: But, honey, think rationally. Why would the government go to such enormous expense and intentionally do something as brutal as what's happened to Nidal, just to punish one former soldier?

DARWIN: It's not punishment. It's tribute. I must pay. They need to know who's on board. I don't think they did this to her to get to me. Don't be ridiculous. It probably just happened. Their experiment failed. But it's perfect for something else. They have to get rid of her. Why not use it as an opportunity to test the loyalty of one who had failed them before?

JO: Darwin, you're really frightening me.

DARWIN: You should be frightened. That's an appropriate response.

JO: She's a human being.

DARWIN: She's a freak.

JO: Nidal has a heart and a mind, Darwin.

DARWIN: Neither of which goes with the same body. And don't forget that brain belongs to an enemy of our country.

NIDAL: I am no one's enemy. I am a doctor. I save lives.

DARWIN: Not yours you don't.

JO: Why did you lie? All these years. To both of us. Why did you fill that boy's head with stories of murder instead of telling him the truth?

DARWIN: I was wrong.

JO: Yes. You should've told me—

DARWIN: No. I mean I was wrong. Back then. I should've followed orders. That was my job. It was my duty to follow the orders of my superiors. I failed.

JO: It wasn't your duty to kill innocent civilians.

DARWIN: It wasn't my responsibility to determine who was innocent.

JO: You can't kill this woman.

DARWIN: *(Takes gun from holster, to* NIDAL*)* "H-U-M—

NIDAL: I will not sign. Whether they think I'm Lucy or Nidal, whether they think I killed myself or not, they will never let you all live.

JO: She's right, Darwin.

DARWIN: *(Picks up box of bullets)* Jo, I've got five hundred bullets here. Don't worry. *(To* NIDAL*)* "H-U-M-P-T-Y...D—umpty! Write it.

NIDAL: I will not.

DARWIN: I'll shoot you.

NIDAL: Then if you wish them to think I did it, you should come and face me.

*(*DARWIN *hesitates, then crosses in front of her.* NIDAL *lifts her face and puts her finger to a point between her eyes.)*

NIDAL: Right here?

*(*DARWIN *puts the gun to her head.)*

JO: *(Fearfully)* Darwin.

*(*NIDAL *looks into* DARWIN*'s eyes. He starts to falter.)*

NIDAL: I am ready when you are, Mister Smith.

RONNIE: *(Apparently disappointed)* Dad.

*(*DARWIN *suddenly turns away from* NIDAL *and puts the gun on the table. He runs out of the room.* JO *follows him.)*

JO: *(Following)* Darwin!

(There is a moment as RONNIE *realizes that* NIDAL *is going to go for the gun. He sprints across the room as she gets to her feet. He gets to the table just behind her, grabs the gun out of her hand, and throws her to the floor.)*

(Offstage, we hear JO *pounding on a door and calling out:)*

JO: *(O S)* Darwin, open the door!

*(*RONNIE *holds the gun, looks down at* NIDAL.*)*

*(*JO *runs into the room, sees* RONNIE *with the gun.)*

JO: Ronnie, go put that away somewhere.

RONNIE: Where?

JO: I don't know. Just hide it!

RONNIE: Okay Mom.

*(*JO *exits hurriedly.)*

JO: *(O S)* Honey! Please let me in.

NIDAL: Please put that down.

*(*RONNIE *doesn't respond, keeps pointing it at her.)*

NIDAL: I am not a threat to you.

(Throughout this next section of dialogue, RONNIE *pursues* NIDAL, *backing her down onto the couch. He will eventually end up forcing her down on her back as he climbs on top of her.)*

RONNIE: Then why'd you go for the gun?

NIDAL: I just wanted to unload it. I was afraid.

RONNIE: You should be.

NIDAL: I understand that you are upset. But you don't want to do something that you will regret.

RONNIE: I'm not a kid.

NIDAL: I know that. But you are a young man with a very promising future. You don't want to do anything to jeopardize that.

RONNIE: How come you speak English so good?

NIDAL: I was educated here.

RONNIE: I didn't think you guys let women go to school.

NIDAL: In my family it was not like that. My father is a doctor. My mother, also, is a teacher.

RONNIE: Bullshit.

(RONNIE *is by now on top of her and drawing his face closer to* NIDAL'*s.)*

NIDAL: What do you have difficulty believing? That we don't all ride camels or that my father has a better job than yours?

RONNIE: Shut the fuck up.

(RONNIE *kisses her roughly. He stops when he realizes she isn't fighting him.)*

(NIDAL *slowly starts to unbutton her blouse.)*

RONNIE: What are you doing?

NIDAL: You wish to rape me. I won't struggle. *(She exposes her breasts to him.)* Take what you want.

(Shamed, RONNIE *touches her hand and pulls her blouse together.)*

NIDAL: What's wrong? You don't want me without violence?

(RONNIE *is suddenly angry. He makes a fist.)*

*(*JO *runs into the room.)*

JO: *(Entering)* Ronnie, you've got to help me—

*(*RONNIE *jumps off couch, hiding gun behind his back.)*

JO: Why were you on top of her?

RONNIE: I wasn't.

(Doorbell)

JO: Lincoln. Ronnie get the door. *(To* NIDAL*)* Get up.

*(*JO *exits.* RONNIE *hides the gun under his clothes and answers the door.)*

JO: *(O S)* Darwin, Commander Lincoln is here. You must come out.

RONNIE: *(Saluting)* Come in, sir.

LINCOLN: *(Entering)* I need to speak to your parents immediately.

RONNIE: Sir, yes, sir. *(Calling offstage)* Mom! Dad! Get out here!

NIDAL: Commander, I'm ready to go. Please.

LINCOLN: It's all been taken care of, Lucy.

*(*JO *and* DARWIN *enter. He looks ill. They join* LINCOLN *at the table.* RONNIE *stands behind* LINCOLN.*)*

JO: Thanks for getting back to us so quickly, Commander Lincoln.

LINCOLN: *(To* DARWIN*)* Are you well, sir?

DARWIN: I vomited.

LINCOLN: Of course. *(To* JO*)* This woman is not your daughter. In fact, it has come to my attention that you don't even have a daughter. I'll put aside for the moment the question of why you chose to deceive the United States government in this matter. There are other issues to deal with right now. *(Opens file)* First of all, it seems that there was a clerical error at the Pentagon which caused you to be misidentified as the parents of Corporal Lucy Smith. Corporal Smith, in fact, has no parents, having been born and raised in an orphanage in Cheyenne, Wyoming. It seems that a rather more significant error occurred in regard to Corporal Smith's accident. When members of the Medivac team arrived at the rescue site, they found one decapitated body and two severed heads. Not wanting to run the risk of potentially getting the wrong head, the team member put both of them in cryo packs and transported them, along with the body, to headquarters. There the head of Corporal Smith was correctly identified by her commanding officer. Both heads were labeled. Lucy's was supposed to go with her body and the other head was to be shipped back state-side to be used for medical research. Unfortunately—

JO: They mixed up the labels.

LINCOLN: Two days ago, an observant research assistant noticed that the head in their cryo storage facility didn't match the description on the label and reported this to Central Security.

DARWIN: So you mean to tell us that Lucy Smith's head has been sitting somewhere on a shelf all this time because of a clerical error?

*(*LINCOLN *ignores this question. He produces a form for* DARWIN *and* JO *to sign.)*

LINCOLN: All I need is for the two of you to sign this form whereby you re-release the body to my custody and swear that you will not divulge any information about these events under penalty of death.

JO: What will happen to Nidal?

LINCOLN: That's not something you need to be concerned with, ma'am.

JO: We're not going to sign anything until you assure us that you're not going to kill this woman.

LINCOLN: Ma'am, I understand that you may have formed a certain emotional attachment to this person, but you can't let that blind you to the truth.

NIDAL: You are blind, Lincoln. They're the impostors. They're plotting to kill you and blackmail the government.

JO: Don't be ridiculous.

NIDAL: *(To* LINCOLN*)* The boy has a gun in his pocket.

*(*LINCOLN *turns. They all look at* RONNIE. *He takes the gun out.)*

JO: Ronnie, I told you to put that away.

*(*RONNIE *points the gun at* NIDAL.*)*

RONNIE: *(To* NIDAL*)* He knows I won't shoot him. He and I are on the same team.

JO: Ronnie, put that gun down.

DARWIN: Listen to her, son. Please. *(Looks at* JO*)* She's right.

*(*RONNIE *looks at* LINCOLN. LINCOLN *opens his file.)*

LINCOLN: She is a terrorist. She's responsible for the deaths of seventeen American soldiers.

*(*LINCOLN *takes a photograph out of the file. He shows it first to* RONNIE, *then to* DARWIN *and* JO.*)*

LINCOLN: Including this one.

*(*JO *looks at* NIDAL.*)*

RONNIE: Why did they chop off your head?

LINCOLN: *(Urgently)* Classified!

NIDAL: *(To* RONNIE*)* Put the gun down and I'll tell you.

LINCOLN: Don't do it, son.

(RONNIE *lowers the gun.)*

NIDAL: I am a doctor. I was taken from my hospital. They told me I was needed for an experiment.

LINCOLN: That is a lie.

NIDAL: *(To* RONNIE*)* It is the truth.

LINCOLN: *(To* RONNIE, *explosively)* Son, this person is an enemy of your country! If she tries to escape, you will shoot to kill!

RONNIE: Sir, yes, sir!

JO: No, Ronnie! Don't listen to him!

NIDAL: *(Standing, to* RONNIE*)* I am innocent.

(Suddenly NIDAL *jumps and sprints toward the door.)*

LINCOLN: Now!

JO: NO!

(RONNIE *fires.* NIDAL *falls to the floor. There is a moment of silence as everyone freezes.* LINCOLN *looks at* RONNIE, *nods, walks straight to the front door and exits.* RONNIE *looks at his parents, drops the gun on the floor. He exits toward the back of the house.* DARWIN *and* JO *look at the dead body on their living room floor, then at each other. Blackout)*

Scene Five

(Lights up. JO *is putting dinner on the table. Her demeanor is subdued and introspective.)*

(Phone rings)

JO: Hello? Hi Patty. How are you? Good. We're okay. *(Listens)* No, Patty, I didn't see it. I haven't been watching the news. *(Listens)* I'm okay. It's just been a rough couple of weeks. *(Listens)* No. Everything's fine. Can I maybe call you later? *(Listens)* Thanks. I love you too. Bye.

(JO hangs up the phone. DARWIN enters.)

JO: Hello.

DARWIN: How was your day?

JO: *(Attempting humor)* Well, like, you know, I'm totally like frightened for and by the youth of America, y'know?

(DARWIN smiles.)

JO: How about you?

DARWIN: *(Suppressing emotion)* I'm afraid I have some bad news. I lost my job today, Jo.

(JO stops what she's doing. She looks at him in disbelief.)

JO: No.

DARWIN: I'm sorry.

(JO crosses to DARWIN and puts her arms around him.)

JO: It's okay, honey. It's okay.

DARWIN: Twenty-three years.

JO: I know.

DARWIN: What am I gonna do?

JO: We'll be okay.

DARWIN: How?

JO: We'll be okay.

DARWIN: Ronnie...

JO: Ronnie will be fine. We have each other. We'll all be fine.

DARWIN: How are we going to send him to college?

JO: We'll figure that out. Come sit down.

*(*JO *leads* DARWIN *to the table and helps him sit down.)*

DARWIN: *(Angrily)* Those dirty sons-of-bitches.

JO: Darwin, please. Try to calm yourself. Ronnie will be home any minute. You don't want him to see you like this.

DARWIN: *(Angrily)* What the hell is happening to this country?

JO: Honey.

DARWIN: I'm sorry.

JO: It's okay.

*(*RONNIE *enters in his baseball uniform. He wears his cap backwards and a pair of cool shades. He throws his cleats on the kitchen counter, and looks at his parents with no emotion, completely detached, ice cold.* DARWIN *and* JO *are anxious, perhaps even afraid.)*

RONNIE: What's up?

DARWIN: Not much, son.

JO: How was your day?

RONNIE: *(Shrugs)* All right.

*(*RONNIE *turns and opens the fridge. He grabs a can of beer and a sausage, closes the fridge, then stands there eating and drinking.* DARWIN *and* JO *both look nervous, but don't say anything about the beer.)*

DARWIN: How was the game?

RONNIE: *(Chews)* Threw a no hitter.

DARWIN: Good going, champ. I wish I could've been there.

JO: I hope Sasha Hurley was watching in the stands.

*(*RONNIE *just looks at her, takes a bite of sausage and a drink of beer.)*

RONNIE: No, Mom. Actually it was a scout from the university.

JO: Oh.

DARWIN: Cool.

RONNIE: *(Chews)* He came up and talked to me afterwards.

DARWIN: Yeah?

RONNIE: *(Drinks, shrugs)* Offered me a scholarship.

JO: Oh honey that's great!

*(*RONNIE *belches.)*

*(*DARWIN *crosses, extends his hand.)*

DARWIN: I'm proud of you, son.

*(*RONNIE *just looks at him with a dismissive sneer, walks past him.)*

RONNIE: *(To* JO*)* When's dinner? I'm starving.

JO: Go get washed up. We'll be ready to eat in just a minute.

*(*RONNIE *walks off toward the back of the house.* DARWIN *and* JO *watch him go.)*

JO: He's going to be fine.

DARWIN: Yes. I'm sure he'll be very successful.

*(*DARWIN *looks at the carpet where* NIDAL *fell after being shot in the previous scene.)*

DARWIN: They did a good job.

JO: *(While setting table)* Who's that?

DARWIN: The carpet cleaners.

*(*JO *looks up at him. Her face grows dark.)*

JO: Yes.

DARWIN: You'd never know.

*(*JO *looks at* DARWIN. *He stares at the floor.)*

(Lights fade to black.)

END OF PLAY

www.ingramcontent.com/pod-product-compliance
Ingram Content Group UK Ltd.
Pitfield, Milton Keynes, MK11 3LW, UK
UKHW020136250726
13967UKWH00002B/688

9 780881 453096